FROM SEA to SHINING SEA

OHIO

NANCY KLINE

Consultants

MELISSA N. MATUSEVICH, PH.D.

Curriculum and Instruction Specialist
Blacksburg, Virginia

BONNIE HOLLAND

Northwest Library Manager
Worthington, Ohio

NANCY J. SMITH

Youth Services Librarian
Youth Services Library Manager
Westerville, Ohio

CHILDREN'S PRESS®

A DIVISION OF SCHOLASTIC INC.

New York • Toronto • London • Auckland • Sydney • Mexico City
New Delhi • Hong Kong • Danbury, Connecticut

Ohio is part of the midwestern United States. It is bordered by Michigan, Indiana, Kentucky, West Virginia, Pennsylvania, and Lake Erie.

The front cover photo shows the skyline of Cincinnati, with a paddle boat in the foreground.

Project Editor: Meredith DeSousa
Art Director: Marie O'Neill
Photo Researcher: Marybeth Kavanagh
Design: Robin West, Ox and Company, Inc.
Page 6 map and recipe art: Susan Hunt Yule
All other maps: XNR Productions, Inc.

Library of Congress Cataloging-in-Publication Data

Kline, Nancy, 1955-
     Ohio / Nancy Kline.
       v. cm. — (From sea to shining sea)
     Includes bibliographical references and index.
     Contents: Introducing the Buckeye state — The land of Ohio — Ohio through history
— Governing Ohio — The people and places of Ohio — Ohio almanac — Timeline —
Gallery of famous Ohioans — Glossary.
  ISBN 0-516-22483-2
     1. Ohio—Juvenile literature. [1. Ohio.] I. Title. II. Series.
F491.3 .K475 2002
977.1—dc21   2001008327

TABLE of CONTENTS

CHAPTER ONE

INTRODUCING THE BUCKEYE STATE

Fireworks light up the sky over Cincinnati, one of Ohio's biggest cities.

Ohio is the "heart of it all." From wild roller coasters to lazy rivers, from amazing science centers to world-class zoos, Ohio has it all. With a mix of cities and agricultural areas, Ohio is an exciting place to work and vacation.

Even the state's earliest settlers found it appealing. *Ohio* is a Native American word meaning "great river." Native Americans used the word in reference to the Ohio River, which forms the state's southeastern and southern borders.

Ohio's nickname is the Buckeye State. During pioneer times, Ohio was known for its buckeye trees. The seeds falling from the trees looked like the eyes of a buck (male) deer, thus the name "buckeye trees." These trees inspired Ohio's nickname. Ohio is also sometimes called the Mother of Presidents. Seven United States presidents were born in

Ohio, and an eighth president lived in Ohio. More presidents came from Ohio than any other state except Virginia.

What comes to mind when you think of Ohio?

- The Wright brothers building the world's first motor-powered airplane
- Ohioan Neil Armstrong walking on the moon
- The world's largest Amish population
- The world's longest wooden roller coaster
- Caverns with rare cave pearls
- Huge burial mounds built by Native Americans
- Fans cheering for the Cincinnati Reds
- The Rock and Roll Hall of Fame in Cleveland

Ohio's history includes people from many backgrounds and cultures. Over time, its people have brought about many of our nation's "firsts." Turn the page to discover the exciting story of Ohio.

Michigan

LAKE ERIE

Toledo

Cleveland

Pennsylvania

Columbus

Indiana

OHIO RIVER

Cincinnati

West Virginia

Kentucky

©SHY02

CHAPTER TWO

THE LAND OF OHIO

Ohio is one of the midwestern states. It is shaped like a square with a dip on the top and a point on the bottom. It is a small state. Only fourteen other states are smaller than Ohio.

Ohio is bordered by five states and a lake. To the west lies Indiana. Pennsylvania is to the east, and West Virginia is to the southeast. Along Ohio's southern border is Kentucky. To the north, Ohio is bordered by Michigan and Lake Erie, one of the five Great Lakes on the United States–Canada border. Also four islands in Lake Erie belong to Ohio: Kelleys Island and the three Bass Islands. Islands are land areas that are completely surrounded by water.

Thousands of years ago the land and the weather in Ohio were very different from what they are today. During what was known as the Ice Age—more than 18,000 years ago—glaciers bulldozed their way across a large part of Ohio. Glaciers are large bodies of ice that move slowly

Farmland covers much of Ohio.

7

across a wide area of land, often flattening hills and scooping out holes along their path. As the glaciers melted, they left mostly flatlands of rich soil. Only the lower part of southeastern Ohio and a small section of land in south-central Ohio were left untouched by the glaciers. As a result of the glacier's movement, Ohio has four land regions. These are the Appalachian Plateaus, the Lake Plain, the Till Plains, and the Bluegrass Region.

APPALACHIAN PLATEAUS

This farm, located in Pike County, sits in the western part of the Appalachian Mountains.

The Appalachian Plateaus cover the eastern part of the state. This region is divided into two areas. The northeast area was flattened by the glaciers. The southeast area has rolling hills left untouched by the glaciers.

Before glaciers passed through, the eastern side of Ohio was covered with rugged mountains. The glaciers stopped before they reached the southern two-thirds of eastern Ohio. As a result, this section is the most rugged part of the state, with steep hills and valleys. These hills and valleys are the Appalachian Mountains. In the United States, only the Rocky Mountains are larger than the Appalachian Mountains in Ohio.

The Appalachians were formed nearly 230 million years ago and are the oldest mountains in North America. The hills in this area rise about 300 to 600 feet (91 to 183 meters) above the valleys.

The soil in this area is thin and not good for growing crops. There are, however, rich mineral deposits of clay, coal, natural gas, oil, and salt in the rugged Appalachian Plateaus.

Port Clinton, situated on the shore of Lake Erie, is a great place for fishing, boating, or relaxing on the beach.

LAKE PLAIN

The northern part of Ohio is an area referred to as the Lake Plain. It is a narrow strip of land that borders Lake Erie. Because of its location, this region is one of the busiest manufacturing, shipping, trading, and recreational areas in the United States. This area also has rich soil and is an excellent place for growing fruits and vegetables. The most heavily populated part of Ohio, the Cleveland metropolitan area, is in the Lake Plain region.

Kelleys Island and the three Bass Islands are also in this region. Kelleys Island has a natural national landmark called Glacial Grooves Memorial. More than 30,000 years ago, glaciers carved through this area and left a gash in the bedrock that is 400 feet (122 m) long and 35 feet (11 m) wide. Kelleys Island is also home to the famous Inscription Rock, which has traces of prehistoric Indian carvings. All four islands are used chiefly as resort areas.

The natural beauty of Kelleys Island makes it a popular resort area.

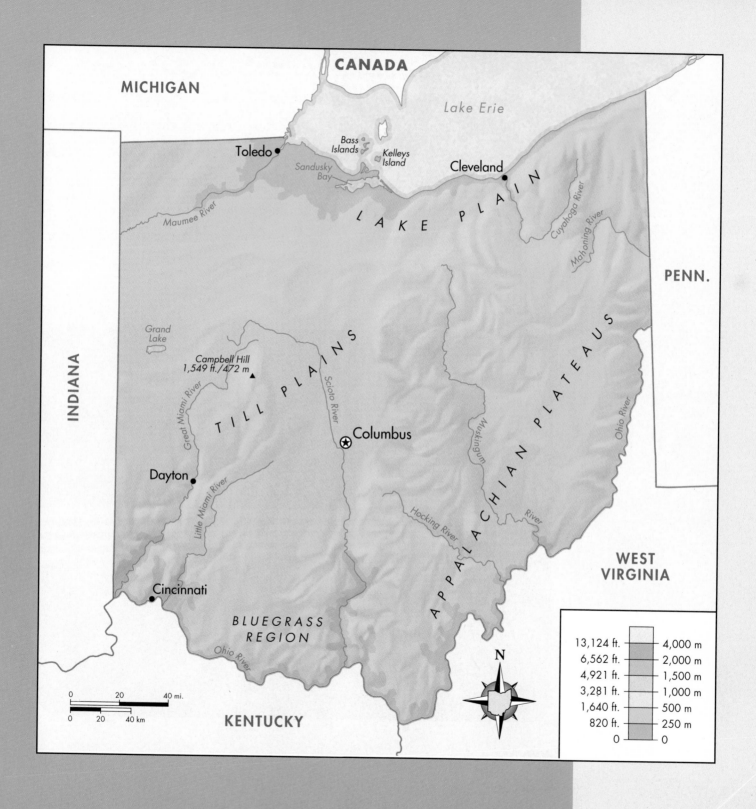

CANADA

MICHIGAN

Lake Erie

Bass Islands

Toledo •

Kelleys Island

Cleveland •

Sandusky Bay

Maumee River

L A K E   P L A I N

Cuyahoga River

Mahoning River

PENN.

INDIANA

Grand Lake

Campbell Hill
1,549 ft./472 m ▲

T I L L   P L A I N S

Great Miami River

Scioto River

Little Miami River

Dayton •

Columbus ⊛

A P P A L A C H I A N   P L A T E A U S

Muskingum

Ohio River

Hocking River

River

WEST VIRGINIA

Cincinnati •

BLUEGRASS REGION

Ohio River

0   20   40 mi.

0   20   40 km

KENTUCKY

N

13,124 ft.	4,000 m
6,562 ft.	2,000 m
4,921 ft.	1,500 m
3,281 ft.	1,000 m
1,640 ft.	500 m
820 ft.	250 m
0	0

The Till Plains region is located south of the Lake Plain in west-central Ohio. Glaciers left most of this land flat, creating deep beds of clay, sand, and gravel in some places. It's not completely flat, however—this area has the highest and lowest points in Ohio. Campbell Hill, near central Ohio, is 1,549 feet (472 m) above sea level. From there the land gradually slopes downward to the southwestern corner of the state in Hamilton County. This area is only 455 feet (139 m) above sea level, the lowest point in Ohio.

Much of Ohio's corn is grown around Marion County, located in the Till Plains.

The Till Plains also ranks among the most fertile farming areas in the country. It is located on the eastern edge of what is called the Corn Belt, an area that produces much of the United States' corn crop. The Corn Belt crosses nine states, including Ohio. The long, hot, and humid summers in this area make it ideal for growing corn. In addition, farmers in the Till Plains produce grain and soybeans and raise livestock.

BLUEGRASS REGION

There is a second, small area along the Ohio River that glaciers did not cover years ago. This triangular area in southern Ohio is an extension of the Bluegrass Region of Kentucky. The region's gentle hills are subject to erosion, where running water and the wind have taken away the fertile topsoil.

RIVERS AND LAKES

Ohio is separated from West Virginia and Kentucky by the Ohio River, one of the longest rivers in North America. The Ohio River is part of a long river system that includes the Allegheny and the Monongahela Rivers. It begins near Pittsburgh, Pennsylvania, and runs 981 miles (1,579 km) before flowing into the Mississippi River at Cairo, Illinois. The Ohio River forms the southern border of Ohio and Indiana and the northern border of West Virginia.

The city of Cincinnati was built along the Ohio River.

A series of low hills that lies along the southern boundary of the Lake Plain divides the rivers that flow to the south and to the north. Rivers that flow north into Lake Erie include the Maumee, Portage, Sandusky, Cuyahoga, and Grand Rivers. The Muskingum, Scioto, Hocking, Mahoning, and Great and Little Miami flow south into the Ohio River.

Ohio also has more than 2,500 lakes larger than 2 acres (0.8 hectares). More than 20 are natural lakes with an area of at least 40 acres (16 ha). Ohio also has more

EXTRA! EXTRA!

Some underground streams in Ohio have helped to form caverns, or caves. Two large caverns in Ohio are the Seven Caves, near Bainbridge, and Ohio Caverns, near West Liberty.

than 180 artificially created lakes that cover at least 40 acres (16 ha) each. Many of these were dug to supply water for canals (manmade ditches that are filled with water) in the late 1800s. Ohio's largest lake is Grand Lake, in northwestern Ohio. It covers 13,500 acres (5,463 ha). Grand Lake was created in the 1840s, when two nearby creeks were dammed to provide water for the Miami and Erie Canal. Another large lake in Ohio is the Pymatuning Reservoir.

CLIMATE

Ohio has hot, humid summers and cold, dry winters. In summer, the average temperature is 84° Fahrenheit (29° Celsius). The average July temperature is 73°F (23°C). The highest recorded temperature was 113°F (45°C) near Gallipolis on July 21, 1934. In January, the average temperature is 28°F (–2°C). The lowest recorded temperature occurred at Milligan on February 10, 1899, when the temperature plunged to –39°F (–39.4°C).

The average rainfall is 38 inches (97 centimeters) in Columbus and 37 inches (94 cm) in Cleveland. The wettest area is in southwest Ohio, where the yearly precipitation is 44 inches (112 cm). The driest part of Ohio is along Lake Erie between Sandusky and Toledo. This area gets only 32

EXTRA! EXTRA!

In the fall, cold air from the north becomes warmer as it passes over Lake Erie, delaying the frost along the shoreline. As a result, the growing season along Lake Erie is 200 days—longer than in the rest of the state. The growing season is the part of a year when it is warm enough for crops to grow; it ends when a strong frost occurs.

Marblehead Lighthouse is surrounded by snow and ice in the winter.

inches (81 cm) of precipitation, including rain and melted snow, each year.

About 2.5 feet (.76 m) of snow falls each year in the state. The eastern and northern parts of Ohio receive the most snow. Northeastern Ohio receives nearly 100 inches (254 cm) of snow annually.

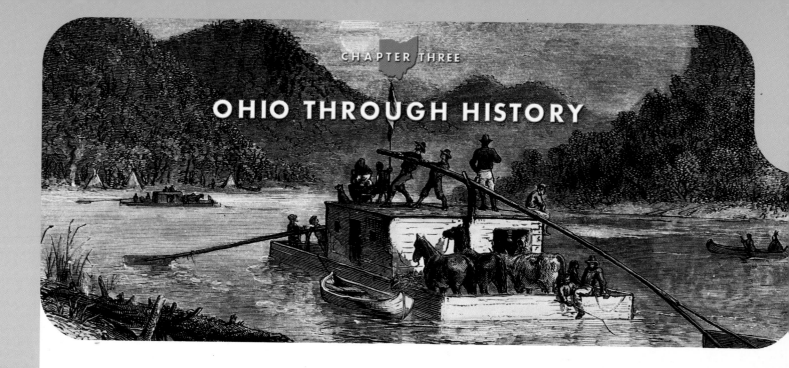

CHAPTER THREE

OHIO THROUGH HISTORY

Paleo-Indians were the first inhabitants of the land we now call Ohio. They first inhabited the area around 12,000 B.C., when glaciers still covered the northern and western parts of what is now Ohio. Paleo-Indians were nomadic people who never stayed in one place for long. They hunted with spears, killing large animals as well as deer and small game. They also fished and gathered nuts and fruit. As the climate warmed and glaciers melted, forests began to appear on Ohio land. The Paleo-Indians moved north toward the Great Lakes, which were formed by the melting ice of the glaciers.

Over time, more hunters and gatherers, called the Archaic people, came to live on Ohio lands. They did not move from place to place like the Paleo-Indians, but settled down in small communities. The Archaic people lived in tents made from wooden poles covered with bark or ani-

During the 1800s, many settlers traveled by boat on the Ohio River.

mal skins. They hunted large and small animals, and fished in the lakes and streams. Some of the fish they caught were smoked and stored for eating during the winter.

When the Ice Age ended, the glaciers melted and the climate warmed. During this time of climatic changes, a variety of plants and animals began to thrive. To survive, the people adapted to these changes. They collected more vegetation for food. Their food sources included fish, acorns, berries, and tubers.

The Archaic people used flint to make tools in order to chop down trees, shape wood into canoes, and carve rock into many shapes. They also used flint to trade with distant groups for copper and seashells.

As the culture changed, the Woodland Tradition began. The Woodland people lived in Ohio more than 2,000 years ago. These prehistoric people built permanent villages. They also built large and elaborate burial mounds from earth and stones. Some of the mounds were formed in the likeness of animals and still exist today, such as Serpent Mound in Adams County and Alligator Mound in Licking County.

The Woodland Tradition included people known as the Adena and later the Hopewell. The Adena people were Ohio's first farmers. They grew sunflowers,

EXTRA! EXTRA!

Today, the Miamisburg Mound is the largest conical (cone-shaped) burial mound in the state of Ohio and possibly in the eastern United States. The mound is round at the base and comes to a point on the top. Scientific investigations suggest that the prehistoric Adena people constructed this mound. Built on a bluff 100 feet (30 m) high, the mound measures 877 feet (267 m) around. It was originally more than 70 feet (21 m) high. Visitors may climb the 116 steps from its base for a view of the surrounding park.

squash, and corn. Hunting and gathering food played an important part in their life.

The Hopewell Indians made weapons for hunting and fighting from copper, shells, animal claws, teeth, and other materials. One of the most important materials they used was the colored flint from Flint Ridge. They lived in small villages in the valleys of southern and central Ohio.

It is believed that Serpent Mound was built between 800 B.C. and A.D. 1200.

Early Native Americans in Ohio harvested maize, or corn.

The Hopewell continued the mound-building tradition begun by the Adena people before them. People from different villages worked together to build grave mounds and enclosures. Their earthworks were larger and shaped like circles, squares, octagons, parallel lines, and other forms. These earthworks were used as places to hold ceremonies. The Hopewell gathered there to worship, trade, and hold social gatherings.

Around A.D. 800, the Woodland people began living in Ohio. They used bows and arrows for hunting. The Woodland people also began to grow corn.

The last of Ohio's early inhabitants reached the area by about A.D. 1000. These included the Fort Ancient people in southern Ohio, the

Whittlesey in northeastern Ohio and the Sandusky in northwestern Ohio. They lived in large villages surrounded by a stockade. Sometimes they built their villages on a plateau overlooking a river.

From the 1600s to the 1800s, the Iroquois from surrounding areas began to push their way into the rich Ohio country because they wanted more land for hunting and trapping beaver and deer. Although the Iroquois were interested in Ohio only for hunting, they drove out native tribes of the Ohio Valley. Then, as the Iroquois grew less powerful, other Native American groups from the east and south moved into Ohio, including the Shawnee, the Delaware, the Wyandot, and the Miami.

EUROPEAN INTERESTS

French explorer René Robert Cavelier, Sieur de La Salle was probably the first European to arrive in present-day Ohio. He may have explored the Ohio River as early as 1669. France claimed Ohio as a French territory based on his travels.

In the meantime, England was settling colonies along the Atlantic coast. As the coastal colonies became crowded, however, the people began looking west. In 1747, English settlers in Virginia formed the Ohio Company. This company hoped to settle Ohio and trade with the Native Americans there for fur. At the time, fur was extremely valuable in Europe, where it was used to make fashionable clothes and hats.

Sieur de La Salle may have traveled down the Ohio River in search of a water passage through North America.

The French and Indian War was largely fought to gain control of the fur trade in the New World.

As more and more fur trading took place, the British (English) and the French began competing for the fur trade. Tensions mounted as the rivalry continued. In 1754, Britain and France went to war to determine who would control the fur trade in the New World, including the land of Ohio. The French and Indian War (1754–1763) ended with the British victorious. Ohio, along with most of the New World, came under British rule.

It wasn't long before war broke out again, this time between the American colonists and Britain. The colonists fought the American Revolution (1776–1783) to gain independence from Britain. The colonists won, and the United States was born. When the war ended, Britain gave up its claim to all land northwest of the Ohio River. In 1787, the United States organized this region—which included Ohio—into what was called the Northwest Territory.

FIND OUT MORE

The Northwest Territory was a very large area of land that was later divided into six states: Ohio, Indiana, Illinois, Michigan, Wisconsin, and part of Minnesota. Draw a map of the Northwest Territory.

EARLY SETTLEMENTS

In 1786, the second Ohio Company was formed to create the first settlement in

Ohio. Two years later, General Rufus Putnam led about 50 men from New England into southeastern Ohio. These men founded Marietta, Ohio's first permanent European settlement. Putnam was placed in charge of the settlement.

In the late 1700s, thousands of people from the eastern states and Kentucky settled in Ohio. American settlers thought they owned the Ohio country, but Native Americans thought the land north of the Ohio River belonged to them. They fought desperately to keep it.

These differences led to fighting between the settlers and Native Americans. In 1782, a group of Native Americans lived in a Christian Indian village called Gnadenhutten. After several white settlers were attacked nearby, the Native Americans were falsely accused of the crime. On March 9, settlers wanted revenge and murdered 96 Native Americans in the village, including 39 children. This event became known as the Gnadenhutten Massacre.

During the late 1700s, Native Americans made several successful attacks on American army posts. However, they also suffered some terrible defeats. On August 20, 1794, General "Mad Anthony" Wayne defeated the Native Americans in the Battle of Fallen Timbers (so named because the battle took place in a forest filled with fallen trees). The two groups would continue to struggle over the next twenty years.

Rufus Putnam was one of the founders of Marietta in 1788.

The Native Americans suffered a terrible defeat at the Battle of Fallen Timbers near Toledo.

STATEHOOD

American settlers continued to clear trees, build cabins, and create settlements in Ohio. By 1803, Ohio had about 70,000 residents, enough to apply for statehood. The United States government granted statehood to Ohio on March 1, 1803, making it the nation's seventeenth state.

Chillicothe served as Ohio's first capital until 1810, when it was moved to Zanesville. The capital returned to Chillicothe in 1812, where it remained until Columbus became Ohio's permanent capital in 1816.

Tecumseh was a Shawnee chief who fought to protect Native American land.

FIGHTING FOR THE LAND

Although Ohio had achieved statehood, problems remained between white settlers and Native Americans. After the Battle of Fallen Timbers, many Native American leaders signed a treaty, or agreement, called the Treaty of Greenville, in 1795. This treaty forced Native Americans to move to the northwestern part of Ohio.

One Native American leader, Tecumseh, refused to sign the treaty. He believed the Ohio lands belonged to Native Americans, and that signing a treaty with the settlers would mean Native Americans would have to give up their way of life. Tecumseh also believed that Native Americans had an obligation to prevent settlers from moving onto the land. Tecumseh worked to unite the tribes so they could fight back.

In 1808, Tecumseh and his brother, who was called the Prophet, left the area and established a town in Indiana called Prophetstown. The Prophet rejected all white ways and encouraged a return to the pure ways of the Native Americans. He worked for peace among the different tribes. Many Native Americans came to live in Prophetstown and shared the dream of one united nation.

Meanwhile, the American settlers became concerned about the uniting of Native Americans. In 1811, before Tecumseh left Prophetstown, he warned his brother not to fight with the settlers. However, the Prophet did not listen and ordered an attack on United States army troops that were stationed nearby. General William Henry Harrison was the leader of these troops. Harrison's troops were prepared for the attack and they easily defeated the Native Americans in what became known as the Battle of Tippecanoe. Prophetstown was left unprotected, and American troops burned it to the ground. The defeat proved devastating, and few Native Americans were left to follow Tecumseh.

Still, Tecumseh did not give up hope that he could regain the Ohio lands. In 1812 he joined a war between Americans and the British, called the War of 1812 (1812–1815). Both sides wanted control of ocean shipping and the Great Lakes. The Battle of Lake Erie was fought off Ohio's shore.

Native Americans, including Tecumseh, fought on the British side. He hoped that if the British won, they would reward his tribes and return the land to Native Americans. Tecumseh, however, never lived to see the end of the war; he was killed in battle in 1813.

Nine American ships defeated a squadron of six British ships in the Battle of Lake Erie.

On September 10, 1813, the Americans achieved an important victory on Lake Erie. An American fleet led by Oliver Hazard Perry captured six British ships, cutting off the British supply lines and forcing them to abandon Detroit, Michigan. The victory also paved the way for General Harrison's attack on British and Native American forces at the Battle of the Thames.

The Battle of the Thames was the final battle of the War of 1812. The battle took place in Ontario, Canada. The British surrendered, and the Native Americans of the Ohio Valley were defeated. The United States and Great Britain signed the Treaty of Ghent on December 24, 1814. Soon, Indian tribes who had lived in Ohio were forced to move to reservations (land that was set aside, or reserved, by the government for Native Americans) in Kansas and other western territories.

EXTRA! EXTRA!

A large monument in honor of Oliver Hazard Perry was constructed on the Ohio island of Put-in-Bay in Lake Erie. The monument, called Perry's Victory and International Peace Memorial, recalls the many victories by this heroic American soldier.

A GROWING STATE

After the war, many more settlers moved into the Ohio region. Some came by boat along the Ohio River and Lake Erie. Others came by wagon. By 1820, the population had risen to 581,434. Ten years later the population reached 937,903. Most of the early settlers were farmers. They cleared the land and raised crops and livestock to fill their own needs.

This drawing shows a view of Cincinnati in 1810.

Although a network of unpaved roads crossed the state, travel was slow and expensive. In 1825, the state legislature decided to build canals to improve transportation. Canals were large ditches filled with water, making it possible for boats to travel over hilly terrain. Two major canals were built in Ohio. The Ohio and Erie Canal traversed eastern Ohio, running from Lake Erie to the Ohio River. The canal began in Cleveland and ended in Portsmouth. The Miami and Erie Canal crossed western Ohio, from Toledo to Cincinnati.

The canals were built by hand, dug with picks and shovels. Teams of horses and oxen were used to power scoops and pull wagons. The primary work force consisted of Irish, German, and French immigrants who labored on the canal for 30 cents a day, plus food, whiskey, and shelter.

Between 1825 and 1847, about 1,000 miles (1,609 km) of canals were constructed in Ohio. The canals not only carried people and freight, they also served as swimming and fishing holes, and ice rinks in the winter months. The canals served as busy trade routes for more than 25 years.

In 1837, work began on a reservoir to feed the Miami and Erie Canal. Feeder lakes were necessary to maintain the canal's 5-foot (1.5-m) water depth. Grand Lake, covering 13,500 acres (5,463 ha) at its completion in 1845, was the largest manmade lake in the world. Other feeder lakes included Indian Lake, Lake Loramie, and Buckeye Lake.

Huge walls called locks kept the water level of the canals even, allowing ships to pass over hilly terrain.

Although the canals were advantageous for most Ohioans, they caused problems for others. Some residents didn't like having canals built on their land. In May 1843, farmers and residents near Grand Lake grew angry. The farmers had not been paid for the lands claimed by the reservoir, and nearby residents complained of the stink of decaying vegetation. In protest, they tore a ditch through the embankment of the Miami and Erie Canal. It cost the state $17,000 to repair the damage. A major flood in 1913 eventually destroyed many of the canals.

The arrival of the railroad also contributed to the decline of canals. Workers built the first railroad in Ohio in 1838. By the end of 1851, railroad lines connected most of Ohio's major cities. By 1860, Ohio had 2,946 miles (4,741 km) of railroad—more than any other state.

A stone railroad bridge curves over the Ohio River in Bellaire.

The railroads were very important for Ohio's cities and towns. They created thousands of jobs. They were also used to ship Ohio products around the country. In 1860, the largest meat-packing center in the nation was in Cincinnati. Other industries in Ohio included furniture, books, soap, clothing, steam engines, steamboats, ceramics, iron working, and paper manufacturing. The railroads also transported crops from farms in all parts of Ohio.

By 1908, the state had 9,582 miles (15,421 km) of track—the most it would

WHAT'S IN A NAME?

Many names and places in Ohio have interesting origins.

Name	Comes From or Means
Tecumseh	Means "panther crossing the sky," in reference to a meteor that crossed the sky when the Shawnee chief was born
Marietta	Named for Marie Antoinette, queen of France
Columbus	Named for Christopher Columbus
Cleveland	Named after Moses Cleaveland, chief surveyor for the Connecticut Land Company, which established the city in 1796
Scioto	From the Iroquoian word for "deer"
Chillicothe	From the Shawnee word meaning "principal city"

ever have. As the years went by, people began to rely more heavily on highways to ship products. Gradually, hundreds of miles of tracks were abandoned.

By 1860, Ohio's population had grown to 2.4 million people. Ohio was the third most populous state in the nation, after New York and Pennsylvania.

THE CIVIL WAR

In the mid-1800s, trouble began brewing in the United States. The conflict between North and South was largely due to slavery, a practice that began in colonial days. Slavery was the practice of buying and selling African-Americans and forcing them to work without pay. Slaves had no freedom and were usually not allowed to learn how to read and write. They were often harshly punished for disobeying their white masters. In the mid-1800s, white landowners in the South used African-Americans to do hard labor on large farms called plantations. Farming was the main industry in the South, and slaves kept the industry going. Without them, the plantation system would break down.

The northern states, including Ohio, did not allow slavery. In those "free states," African-Americans were free people. Many Ohioans, as well as other northerners, wanted to put an end to slavery.

Many slaves escaped from their owners by fleeing north to Canada. Because Ohio was on the route to Canada, many Ohioans helped slaves to escape along the Underground Railroad. This was not a real railroad; rather, it was a series of hiding places. A well-known hiding place in Ohio was the John Rankin house along the Ohio River. Between 1825 and 1865, Reverend John Rankin sheltered more than 2,000 escaped slaves.

In 1861, the North and the South went to war. This is known as the Civil War (1861–1865). About 345,000 Ohioans fought for the North, but no battles occurred in Ohio until 1863. That year, General John Hunt Morgan led more than 2,000 southern soldiers into Ohio. Ohio militiamen chased Morgan's Raiders until they were captured.

Two great northern generals during the war were Ohioans Ulysses S. Grant and William Tecumseh Sherman. Another famous Ohio soldier was George Armstrong Custer. Custer was

The outside staircase of the Rankin House was sometimes called the "stairway to freedom."

General Morgan's army stormed into Ohio, taking the settlers by surprise.

the brigadier general of volunteers during the Civil War. He fought in many battles. In 1865, the North was victorious, and the nation began to rebuild.

GREAT ACHIEVEMENTS

After the Civil War, Ohio became an important industrial state. Many products were produced in Ohio. Benjamin F. Goodrich began manufacturing rubber in Akron in 1870. In the Toledo area, the glassmaking industry developed. Youngstown made steel. Cincinnati made soap. In 1879,

Ohioan James Ritty invented the cash register, and the National Cash Register Company opened in Dayton in 1884. John D. Rockefeller started the Standard Oil Company in Cleveland. By 1880, Standard Oil owned almost all the oil refineries (factories that turn oil into gasoline and other useful products) in the United States.

As more industries sprang up, the population in Ohio swelled. By 1900, Ohio had more than 4.1 million people. With so many people, it isn't surprising that Ohioans were achieving great things. Wilbur and Orville Wright of Dayton made the first motor-powered airplane. In 1903, Orville Wright made the world's first successful airplane flight, which lasted for twelve seconds. In 1909, Charles F. Kettering of Loudonville developed the first successful self-starter for cars. Kettering's invention made it possible to start cars with a key instead of a hand crank.

Between 1869 and 1923, seven Ohio natives served as president. These were Ulysses S. Grant, Rutherford B. Hayes, James A. Garfield, Benjamin Harrison, William McKinley, William Howard Taft, and Warren G. Harding.

The Wright brothers' first flight took place in Kitty Hawk, North Carolina, on December 17, 1903.

WHO'S WHO IN OHIO?

Ulysses S. Grant (1822–1885) was commander of the Union (Northern) forces during the Civil War. In 1868 he was elected the eighteenth president of the United States and served two terms (1869 to 1877). Grant was born in a two-room cabin in Point Pleasant.

33

WORLD WAR I

World War I (1914–1918) began in Europe in 1914. The United States did not enter the war until 1917, when it joined the European countries of France, England, Italy, and others to fight against Germany and Austria-Hungary. Nearly 250,000 Ohioans fought in this war. Eddie Rickenbacker of Columbus became the leading American combat pilot. He shot down 22 enemy planes and four observation balloons. Before joining the United States Army in 1917, he was an internationally famous race car driver who had won many championships and set a world record for speed driving.

Ohio made other contributions to the war effort. An Ohio lawyer, Newton D. Baker, served as President Woodrow Wilson's secretary of war during World War I. In addition, Ohio's factories made airplanes, trucks, steel, and rubber for use in fighting.

After the war ended in 1918, Ohio enjoyed a brief period of prosperity and industrial growth. This time was known as the Roaring Twenties. It wouldn't last long, however. In 1929, Ohio—and the rest of the country—experienced hard times. Many people lost huge

World War II fighter pilot Eddie Rickenbacker sits in the cockpit of his fighter aircraft.

amounts of money in their business investments, and as a result they found it difficult to make payments on their homes or to buy food and other products. Many businesses couldn't sell their wares and closed down. This was the start of the Great Depression (1929–1939). The depression was especially severe in the centers of Ohio's heavy industry, including Youngstown, Akron, Toledo, and Cleveland. One-third to one-half of the people in Ohio did not have jobs. It wasn't until the late 1930s that the economy finally began to recover because of the start of another war.

In 1939, World War II (1939–1945) began in Europe. The United States did not join the fighting until 1941, when Japan attacked a United States military base at Pearl Harbor, Hawaii. About 838,000 men and women from Ohio served in the armed forces during World War II.

On the home front, many Ohioans worked hard to meet the demands of war. Ohio's agricultural production increased to feed the troops. The mining of coal increased. The production of iron, steel, aircraft parts, ships, tanks, jeeps, and other vehicles also increased. Ohio ranked fourth in war productivity. Thousands of unpaid volunteers served as air-raid wardens (people who watched the sky for enemy planes) and Red Cross workers.

Because of the large number of men in the military and the need for increased productivity, 6.5 million women in the United States entered the work force between 1941 and 1945. Many women were employed in jobs traditionally done by men. Women worked as welders and mechanics. They also produced weapons.

To help the war effort, goods were rationed to people on the home front, including Ohio, to make sure there were enough supplies for the soldiers. Each person was allowed only three pairs of shoes. Food rations included 28 ounces of meat a week and 4 ounces of butter a week per person. Long-distance telephone calls were limited to five minutes. The government ordered the employees of some defense plants to work a minimum of 48 hours a week.

A factory worker assembles gas masks during World War II.

INDUSTRIAL GROWTH

After the war, industrial growth in Ohio continued. Ohio became third among American states in industrial productivity. Between 1951 and 1969, Ohio manufacturers spent more money on new factory plants and equipment than manufacturers in any other state.

Farming in Ohio also changed after World War II. Bigger farm equipment and more effective chemical fertilizers were developed, making it possible for fewer farmers to produce more crops. In 1949, Ohio had 250,000 farms. Thirty years later there were only about 125,000 farms. When Ohio first became a state, most of the families farmed full time. Now, fewer than three percent of Ohio families (3 in every 100 families) are farmers.

This industry growth brought problems, however. During the 1960s, Ohio had serious pollution problems. The state's many cities and factories were ruining the water and the air. Factories regularly dumped waste in the rivers. In 1969, the Cuyahoga River in Cleveland was so full of pollutants that it caught fire. Pollution was also causing fish in Lake Erie to die.

The 1960s was also a difficult time for Ohio's cities. Many people moved out of the cities into the suburbs. Rioting occurred because poor people and African-Americans did not feel they had a voice in government.

Although industrial growth in Ohio continued into the early 1970s, many factories in Ohio were becoming outdated. Also, the cost of running a business was higher in Ohio than in southern and western states.

A stream polluted with waste water flows into the Ohio River.

During this period, energy costs skyrocketed as Ohio's high-quality coal and natural gas resources were depleted.

Across the state, industry after industry closed or drastically cut production. Unemployment soared. From 1972 to 1982, the state lost nearly 250,000 manufacturing jobs. As these jobs drained off to states in the South and the West, the term "rust belt" was increasingly applied to Ohio and other industrial states of the Northeast and the Midwest. This name came from the many empty, rusting buildings that remained standing in the area after the industries closed and moved to other states.

MODERN OHIO

Ohioans worked to solve these problems. Work was done to clean up Ohio's air and water. Laws prevented industries and cities from polluting Ohio's waterways and air. Lake Erie and the Cuyahoga River are now clean enough for people and fish.

Race relations also improved. In 1967, Cleveland elected Carl Stokes as mayor. Stokes, who was the great-grandson of a slave, defeated Seth Taft—great-grandson of a United States president—to become the first African-American mayor of a major United States city.

During the 1980s, Ohio's industries became more modernized. Many were replaced with newer, high-technology industries. By the 1990s, Ohio ranked among the top five manufacturing states, producing automobiles, machinery, computers, chemicals, paper products, plastics, primary and fabricated metal products, and processed food.

Some problems remained, however. In the 1990s, Ohio manufacturers—especially those in the steel industry—faced increasing competition from manufacturers in other countries. Many Ohio farmers also had difficulties. Declining prices for crops and livestock resulted in lower incomes for farmers. Many smaller farmers have been forced out of business. Ohio also lost a large number of people in the work force during this time. From 1990 to 2000, 156,000 people ages 20 through

FAMOUS FIRSTS

- Oberlin College was the first United States college to admit women in 1837
- Oberlin graduate John M. Langston was the first African-American in the United States elected to a public office when he became the clerk of Ottawa Township in 1855
- The first public weather forecasting service was started in Cincinnati on September 1, 1869
- The first electric traffic signal lights were invented by James Hoge of Cleveland; they were installed in Cleveland on August 5, 1914
- The Cincinnati Red Stockings (now the Reds) became the first professional baseball team in 1869

A worker stands by a river of molten steel at a steel company in Ohio.

54 left Ohio. According to the 2000 census, however, the population in Ohio was 11,353,140—an increase of five percent over the 1990 census figure of 10,847,115. Ohio now ranks seventh in population among the states.

Ohio will celebrate its 200th birthday (bicentennial) in 2003. Exciting plans are under way for this celebration. The Ohio Bicentennial Commission is casting bicentennial bells in each of Ohio's 88 counties. (In Ohio's early days, bells were commonly seen in courthouses, schools, and churches.) The commission is also painting at least one barn in every Ohio county with the red, white, and blue bicentennial logo. Ohio's 200th birthday will be a time for the state to celebrate its rich and diverse culture.

This barn in Delaware County is painted with the bicentennial logo.

CHAPTER FOUR

GOVERNING OHIO

Four Civil War cannons are on display outside the Ohio statehouse.

Ohio's **first constitution,** a document outlining the power and duties of the state government, was adopted in 1802. A new constitution was adopted in 1851. This constitution ensured that members of the government would be elected by the people. However, it wasn't until 1967 that Ohio voters approved a constitutional amendment, or change, establishing the three branches (parts) of government that exist today. They are the legislative branch, the executive branch, and the judicial branch.

LEGISLATIVE BRANCH

Known as the general assembly, this branch of government makes laws for the state. The general assembly also allocates money to help pay for schools, build roads, and protect the environment.

The legislative branch has two parts, the house of representatives and the senate. The house of representatives has 99 members. Each representative serves a two-year term and may serve up to four successive terms. There are 33 senators. Each senator is elected to a four-year term and may serve up to two terms. All of the legislators are elected by the people.

Senators gather to discuss Ohio laws inside the state senate chamber, shown below.

EXECUTIVE BRANCH

The executive branch enforces and carries out the laws of the state. The governor, who is elected to a four-year term, is the leader of the executive branch. He or she is responsible for proposing the state budget, signing laws passed by the legislative branch, and appointing leaders to various state offices.

Other members of the executive branch include the lieutenant governor, the secretary of state, the attorney general, the treasurer, and the auditor. The lieutenant governor is a member of the governor's cabinet (staff) and presides at staff meetings in the absence of the governor. The secretary of state is the chief election officer for the state, appointing members of the 88 county boards of elections. The attorney general is the chief law enforcement officer for the state and all its departments. In cases that involve the state of Ohio, members of the attorney general's office appear on behalf of the state.

The treasurer is responsible for collecting, investing, and protecting state money. He or she collects most state taxes and manages this money. The auditor is responsible for checking the business accounts of all public offices in Ohio. All these officers are elected to serve four-year terms.

JUDICIAL BRANCH

The judicial branch interprets the laws. This branch is made up of the court system. It includes the Ohio supreme court, 12 courts of appeals,

OHIO STATE GOVERNMENT

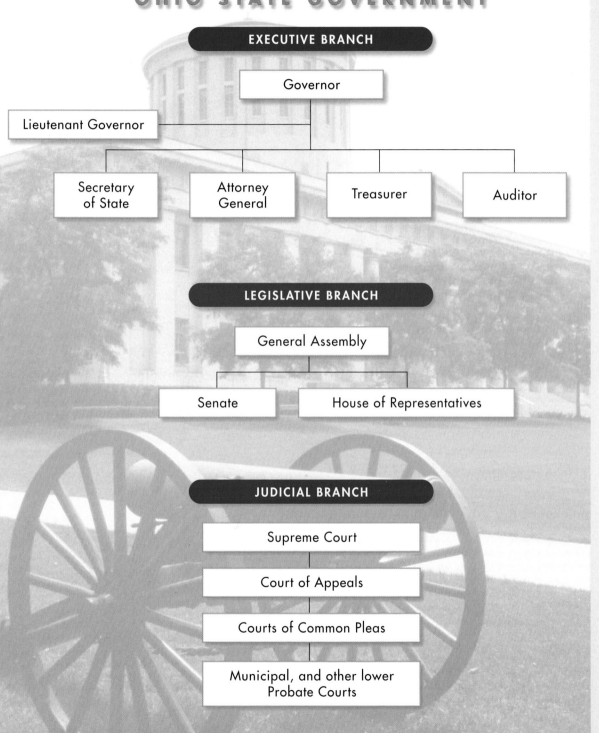

EXECUTIVE BRANCH

Governor

Lieutenant Governor

Secretary of State

Attorney General

Treasurer

Auditor

LEGISLATIVE BRANCH

General Assembly

Senate

House of Representatives

JUDICIAL BRANCH

Supreme Court

Court of Appeals

Courts of Common Pleas

Municipal, and other lower Probate Courts

OHIO GOVERNORS

Name	Term	Name	Term
Edward Tiffin	1803–1807	Richard M. Bishop	1878–1880
Thomas Kirker	1807–1808	Charles Foster	1880–1884
Samuel Huntington	1808–1810	George Hoadly	1884–1886
Return J. Meigs Jr.	1810–1814	Joseph B. Foraker	1886–1890
Othniel Looker	1814	James E. Campbell	1890–1892
Thomas Worthington	1814–1818	William McKinley	1892–1896
Ethan A. Brown	1818–1822	Asa S. Bushnell	1896–1900
Allen Trimble	1822	George K. Nash	1900–1904
Jeremiah Morrow	1822–1826	Myron T. Herrick	1904–1906
Allen Trimble	1826–1830	John M. Pattison	1906
Duncan McArthur	1830–1832	Andrew L. Harris	1906–1909
Robert Lucas	1832–1836	Judson Harmon	1909–1913
Joseph Vance	1836–1838	James M. Cox	1913–1915
Wilson Shannon	1838–1840	Frank B. Willis	1915–1917
Thomas Corwin	1840–1842	James M. Cox	1917–1921
Wilson Shannon	1842–1844	Harry L. Davis	1921–1923
Thomas W. Bartley	1844	A. Victor Donahey	1923–1929
Mordecai Bartley	1844–1846	Myers Y. Cooper	1929–1931
William Bebb	1846–1849	George White	1931–1935
Seabury Ford	1849–1850	Martin L. Davey	1935–1939
Reuben Wood	1850–1853	John W. Bricker	1939–1945
William Medill	1853–1856	Frank J. Lausche	1945–1947
Salmon P. Chase	1856–1860	Thomas J. Herbert	1947–1949
William Dennison Jr.	1860–1862	Frank J. Lausche	1949–1957
David Tod	1862–1864	John W. Brown	1957
John Brough	1864–1865	C. William O'Neill	1957–1959
Charles Anderson	1865–1866	Michael V. DiSalle	1959–1963
Jacob D. Cox	1866–1868	James A. Rhodes	1963–1971
Rutherford B. Hayes	1868–1872	John J. Gilligan	1971–1975
Edward F. Noyes	1872–1874	James A. Rhodes	1975–1983
William Allen	1874–1876	Richard F. Celeste	1983–1991
Rutherford B. Hayes	1876–1877	George V. Voinovich	1991–1999
Thomas L. Young	1877–1878	Robert Taft	1999–

courts of common pleas, county courts, municipal courts, and the court of claims.

There is a court of common pleas in each county. These courts hear cases involving serious crimes such as murder and armed robbery. They also hear civil cases where one person or organization is suing another for more than $500. Common pleas judges are elected to six-year terms. Most courts of common pleas have special divisions to decide cases involving juveniles, estate settlements, and domestic-relation matters such as divorce.

If someone is not satisfied with the court's decision, he or she may appeal the decision, which means to take their case to a higher court. The court of appeals reviews the decisions made in some common pleas, municipal, and county courts.

Some cases that are appealed reach the Ohio supreme court, the state's highest and most important court. The supreme court includes a chief justice (judge) and six other justices who are elected to six-year terms. There is no term limit.

TAKE A TOUR OF COLUMBUS, THE STATE CAPITAL

When Columbus was chosen as the state capital in 1816, it was not yet a town. It was only a plot of land located on the Scioto River. The area for the state capital was chosen because of its central location. It was near a place known as Franklinton, which had been a thriving trade center in

Columbus is the fifteenth largest city in the United States.

Ohio since 1797. Located in Franklin County, Columbus is the largest city in Ohio, with a population of 711,470.

The capitol building, known as the statehouse, is located in the center of Columbus. It was built between 1839 and 1861. Prisoners from the Ohio penitentiary constructed the foundation and ground floors of the building. Limestone for the building was taken from a quarry on the nearby west banks of the Scioto River.

Inside the statehouse, the rotunda (a circular room) is decorated with 28 colors, including nearly 5,000 pieces of hand-cut marble from around the world arranged in the floor. It is 120 feet (37 m) from the floor to the skylight.

The rotunda is one of the most impressive rooms in the statehouse. The painting by William Powell shows a scene from the Battle of Lake Erie.

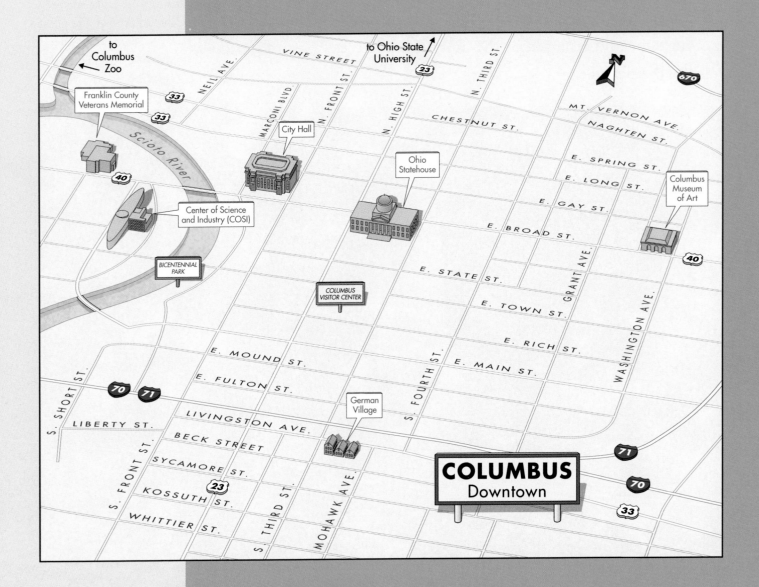

to
Columbus
Zoo

VINE STREET

to Ohio State
University

23

N

670

NEIL AVE.

33

33

Scioto River

40

Franklin County
Veterans Memorial

MARCONI BLVD.

N. FRONT ST.

City Hall

N. HIGH ST.

N. THIRD ST.

CHESTNUT ST.

MT. VERNON AVE.

NAGHTEN ST.

E. SPRING ST.

Columbus
Museum
of Art

Center of Science
and Industry (COSI)

Ohio
Statehouse

E. LONG ST.

E. GAY ST.

40

BICENTENNIAL
PARK

E. BROAD ST.

GRANT AVE.

COLUMBUS
VISITOR CENTER

E. STATE ST.

E. TOWN ST.

WASHINGTON AVE.

E. RICH ST.

S. SHORT ST.

E. MOUND ST.

S. FOURTH ST.

E. MAIN ST.

70 71

E. FULTON ST.

LIBERTY ST.

LIVINGSTON AVE.

German
Village

71

BECK STREET

S. FRONT ST.

SYCAMORE ST.

S. THIRD ST.

MOHAWK AVE.

70

COLUMBUS
Downtown

23

KOSSUTH ST.

33

WHITTIER ST.

The Statehouse Education and Visitors Center is located below a covered passageway, called an atrium, which connects the statehouse and the senate building. Thousands of students who visit the capitol start in the visitors' center to learn about their state government. The center includes a map room containing a map of Ohio that was constructed using six types of marble from around the world.

Outside the statehouse are statues and monuments. Located at the west side of the statehouse, the McKinley Monument was erected in 1906 to honor William McKinley, former governor and United States president. The oldest monument on the grounds, called These Are My Jewels, is located at the northwest corner of the statehouse. It was designed for the World's Columbian Exposition of 1893. The large sculpture along the north side of the statehouse is known as Peace. It was erected in 1923 by the Women's Relief Corps of Ohio in honor of Civil War soldiers.

Also at the statehouse is Veterans Plaza. The plaza honors Ohio men and women who have served our country since World War II, as well as those who will serve in the future. Four cannons, each weighing almost one ton, are on display outside the statehouse. The cannons were manufactured in Cincinnati.

There's lots to see in Columbus besides the capitol. The Columbus area is the site of Ohio State University, where more than 50,000 students attend college. It is the largest educational institution in Ohio.

If you enjoy museums, the Columbus Museum of Art houses one of the nation's best collections of mid-19th- to mid-20th-century Ameri-

Ohio State University was established in 1870. Its first class had only 24 students; today, more than 50,000 students attend the school.

can paintings. It also has a special area for children to enjoy art. The Center of Science and Industry (COSI) in Columbus includes exhibits about science, industry, and history. The center also has three theaters, including a planetarium where computer-generated images and a one-of-a-kind sound system create a sense of realism. The Learning Worlds in COSI allow guests of all ages to experience hands-on learning.

Another leading attraction is the Columbus Zoo and Aquarium. This zoo has a natural-like habitat including a large coral reef aquarium. The African Forest region transports visitors to the rain forests of Africa. Leopards, gorillas, bongo (antelope), mandrills, red river hogs, and colorful birds are among the animals that guests observe.

COSI makes science fun with plenty of hands-on exhibits.

Spring and summer are good times to visit Columbus. Each year between May and September, more than 100 free outdoor music, dance, and drama performances take place in city parks and recreation centers in Columbus. In summer check out the Ohio State Fair, one of the largest state fairs in the country. More than a million visitors attend the fair each year. One of its most unusual attractions is a cow made entirely from butter!

A good place to end your tour of Columbus is German Village. During the early 1800s, many Germans immigrated to Ohio and started communities around Columbus. Although most of the original homes in German Village have been restored, the area's tree-lined brick streets and German-style buildings serve as reminders of the past. You can tour the homes during the last weekend of June, at the annual Haus and Garten Tour.

CHAPTER FIVE

THE PEOPLE AND PLACES OF OHIO

People of many nationalities live in Ohio. According to the 2000 census, the population included 9,614,571 people of European descent, 1,291,939 African-Americans, 94,538 American Indian and Alaskan natives, 146,202 Asians, and 6,296 native Hawaiians and other Pacific Islanders. The largest population groups include people of English, Irish, and German descent. About eleven of every one hundred people in Ohio are African-American. About two in every one hundred people are Hispanic and one in every hundred is Asian American.

About half of Ohio's people live in the state's three largest metropolitan areas—Cincinnati, Cleveland, and Columbus. Columbus ranks as the largest city in Ohio. Five other cities in the state have populations of more than 100,000. They are, in order of size, Cleveland, Cincinnati, Toledo, Akron, and Dayton.

An Amish horse-and-buggy traveling at sunset.

WORKING IN OHIO

For more than 125 years, Ohio has been a leading manufacturing state. Ohio ranks high in the United States in the manufacture of motor vehicles and motor vehicle parts, industrial machinery, food products, and steel. Akron is known for rubber. Cincinnati is known for making jet engines and machine tools. Toledo is known for making glass and auto parts. Office machines, heating equipment, and auto equipment are also produced in Ohio.

Manufacturing jobs make up only part of Ohio's work force. Most of the state's workers are employed in service jobs, including jobs in education, health care, and wholesale and retail trade. Cleveland and Columbus are important financial centers in the United States. Cleveland is home to some of the nation's leading health-care centers. Ohio's third

largest city, Cincinnati, is the home of several major retail companies, including Federated Department Stores and Kroger. Wendy's, a leading restaurant chain, is headquartered in Dublin. The Limited, a major retail clothing chain, is headquartered in Columbus.

In Ohio's early days, the majority of people were farmers. Now, fewer than three in every one hundred Ohioans work in farming jobs. However, Ohio continues to be strong in the amount of crops produced. Farmland covers about half of Ohio. Ohio leads the country in the production of tomato juice and is second only to California in tomato growing. In 1995, Ohio ranked first in the nation in the production of Swiss cheese. Today, soybeans and corn are the leading crops in Ohio's agriculture. In 1995, Ohio ranked fifth in the nation in production of

MICHIGAN

PENN.

Lake Erie

Toledo

Cleveland

INDIANA

Columbus

Dayton

Cincinnati

WEST
VIRGINIA

KENTUCKY

N

0   20   40 mi.

0   20   40 km

Cattle
Clay
Coal
Corn
Dairy
Fruit
Hay
Hogs
Grapes
Gypsum
Limestone
Manufacturing
Natural gas
Oats
Petroleum
Poultry
Salt
Sheep
Soybeans
Sugar beets
Tobacco
Vegetables
Wheat

sweet corn. Ohio also ranks second in the nation in egg production. Egg-producing farms are located in the west-central and east-central parts of the state. Ohio ranks 11th in the production of apples; they are grown in every county in Ohio.

Another major source of employment in Ohio is mining. Ohio is among the top coal-mining states. Deposits in eastern and southeastern Ohio have an estimated 24 billion tons (22 billion metric tons) of coal.

TAKE A TOUR OF OHIO

Northwest Ohio

Let's start our tour in northwestern Ohio on the shores of Lake Erie. There you can enjoy a day of fishing or board a boat to one of the four Ohio islands. The islands are popular vacation spots. Inscription Rock, on Kelleys Island, has 400-year-old Indian carvings. Visitors can also visit the Glacial Grooves, where grooves were carved into rock thousands of years ago by the glaciers that crossed Ohio.

Visitors of all ages will enjoy Cedar Point Amusement Park. This park is home to the largest collection of rides (68) on earth. It has 15 roller coasters (one of which is the world's tallest and fastest double-twisting impulse roller coaster)—more than any other place on Earth!

Ohio is not only a leading apple producer, it is also a major consumer of apples! One of the best ways to enjoy delicious apples is by eating apple dumplings, a popular food in Ohio. Don't forget to ask an adult for help.

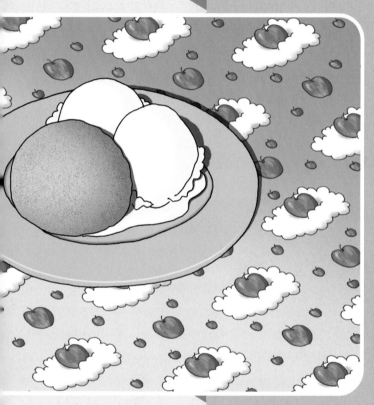

AMISH APPLE DUMPLINGS

One tube (12 oz.) refrigerated buttermilk biscuits
Five medium apples, peeled, cored, and cut in half
3/4 cup brown sugar
3/4 cup water
1/3 cup butter or margarine, melted
1 teaspoon vanilla extract
1/4 teaspoon ground cinnamon

1. Flatten each biscuit with your hand.
2. Place an apple half on each biscuit.
3. Wrap each biscuit around the apple half.
4. Place seam side down in a greased baking dish.
5 Combine sugar, water, butter or margarine, and vanilla extract.
6. Pour the liquid mixture over the pan of dumplings.
7. Sprinkle cinnamon over dumplings.
8. Bake, uncovered, at 350°F for 35-40 minutes or until the dumplings are golden brown and the apples are tender. Serve with milk or ice cream.

West of Cedar Point is the city of Toledo. Toledo is known for the Toledo Zoo, featuring a unique hippoquarium that allows visitors to see hippos swimming underwater. The Toledo Museum of Art features a large collection of glass and European paintings. If you enjoy glass collecting, the U.S. Glass Specialty Outlet, also in Toledo, features glassblowers at work.

The Toledo Zoo Hippoquarium offers visitors a close-up look at a hippo and her newborn calf.

(opposite)
Several cars that were once used onstage at a U2 concert hang from the ceiling at the Rock and Roll Hall of Fame.

Southeast of Toledo is Milan, the birthplace of Thomas Edison. The Edison Birthplace Museum tells the life story of this famous inventor, whose inventions include the light bulb, the record player, and many other items.

Farther south, another museum marks the birthplace of Neil Armstrong, another famous Ohioan. In his honor, the city of Wapakoneta built the Neil Armstrong Air and Space Museum. The museum has a moon rock on exhibit and features videos describing the history of the space program.

Two castles, known as the Piatt Castles, sit in central-western Ohio. General Abram Sanders Piatt and Colonel Donn Piatt built limestone 19th-century castles just outside of West Liberty. Mac-A-

Chee Castle remains the Piatt family home and houses original furnishings, a Native American artifact collection, and a firearms collection. Mac-O-Chee Castle has beautifully painted walls and ceilings and is known for its unique architecture.

Northeast Ohio

Located along Lake Erie, Cleveland is a good place to start our tour of northeast Ohio. Cleveland has many museums, but it is best known for its Rock and Roll Hall of Fame and Museum. The museum includes incredible interactive exhibits, classic films, and rare collectibles including instruments from well-known rock and roll stars.

At the Cleveland Metro Park Zoo, you can watch koalas, kangaroos, and many other animals as

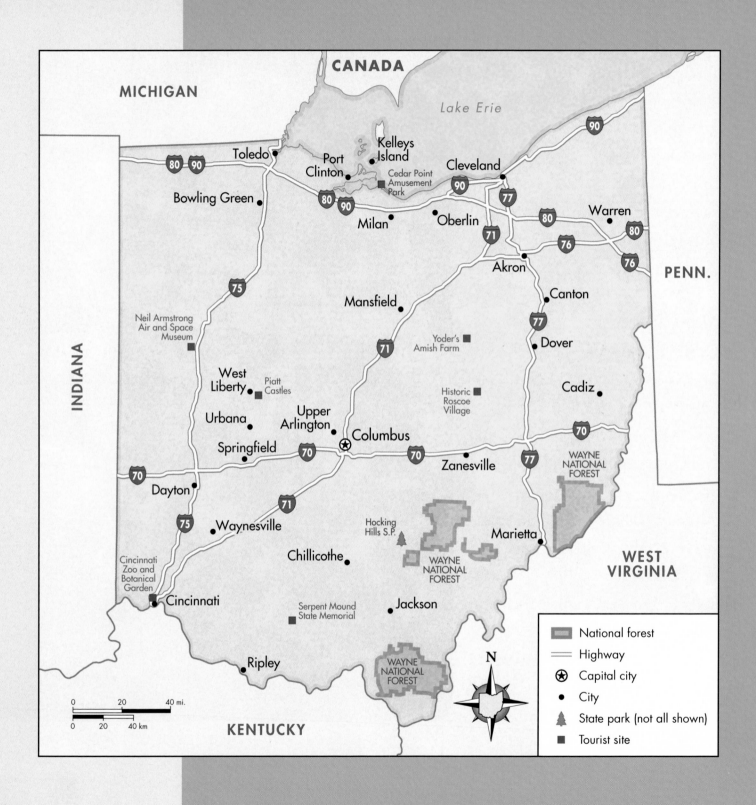

CANADA

MICHIGAN

Lake Erie

Toledo

Port
Clinton

Kelleys
Island

Cleveland

Cedar Point
Amusement
Park

Bowling Green

Milan

Oberlin

Warren

80 90

80 90

90

90

77

80

80

71

76

76

PENN.

Akron

Mansfield

Canton

75

Neil Armstrong
Air and Space
Museum

71

Yoder's
Amish Farm

77

Dover

INDIANA

West
Liberty

Piatt
Castles

Historic
Roscoe
Village

Cadiz

Urbana

Upper
Arlington

70

Columbus

Springfield

70

70

Zanesville

77

70

WAYNE
NATIONAL
FOREST

70

Dayton

71

75

Waynesville

Hocking
Hills S.P.

Marietta

WAYNE
NATIONAL
FOREST

WEST
VIRGINIA

Cincinnati
Zoo and
Botanical
Garden

Chillicothe

Cincinnati

Serpent Mound
State Memorial

Jackson

WAYNE
NATIONAL
FOREST

Ripley

	National forest
	Highway
	Capital city
	City
	State park (not all shown)
	Tourist site

N

0   20   40 mi.

0   20   40 km

KENTUCKY

they roam 165 rolling wooded acres (67 ha). The zoo also includes a "rain forest" that features wildlife from the jungles of Africa, Asia, and the Americas.

In Canton, south of Cleveland, you will find the Pro Football Hall of Fame. The American Professional Football Association was founded in Canton. The museum is a round building with a football-shaped dome. Built in 1963, it holds exhibits covering the history of pro football and features pictures, clothing, and equipment of 200 players who have been inducted into the hall of fame. Game Day Stadium, a state-of-the-art turntable theater, features the film *Championship Chase*. Game Day Stadium delivers the full-force energy of pro football and highlights NFL action.

Farther south you'll find Holmes and Tuscarawas counties, home of the world's largest Amish population. Horse-drawn buggies travel down the roads while horse-drawn plows work in the field. Yoder's Amish Farm is a 116-acre (47-ha) working farm in this area. It includes two homes open to tours, a petting zoo, buggy rides, hayrides, and crafts.

Step back in time with a visit to Historic Roscoe Village, a restored 19th-century canal town. Visitors of all ages will enjoy watching costumed craftspeople and shopkeepers re-create life in the 1820s in this once-bustling port on the Ohio and Erie Canal.

Southeastern Ohio

The Appalachian Mountains are in southeastern Ohio. In Hocking County, you will find scenic Hocking Hills State Park and Hocking State Forest. This area includes hiking trails that take visitors over swinging bridges and ravines and through caves. The visitor center at Old Man's Cave in Hocking Hills State Park features displays about the amazing geology and history of the area.

Ash Cave, located in Hocking Hills State Park, is one of the most spectacular features in Ohio. It is thought that early inhabitants of Ohio once used the cave for shelter.

Tucked into the southeast corner of Ohio, Wayne National Forest lies in the foothills of the Appalachian Mountains. Its rugged hills are covered with diverse stands of hardwoods, pine, and cedar. Lakes, rivers, streams, springs, rock shelters, and covered bridges are all part of Wayne National Forest.

In Hocking Valley near Nelsonville, you can take a train ride on the Hocking Valley Scenic Railway. Climb aboard an old-time passenger train for a leisurely 14-mile (23-km) ride through beautiful Hocking Hills. The National Road–Zane Grey Museum is located near Zanesville. The museum has displays describing the life of Zane Grey.

Located along the Ohio River is the state's oldest town, Marietta. Founded by Rufus Putnam in 1788, the town features the Campus Martius Museum. This center for the history of settlement in Ohio spans the period from 1780 to 1970. The main-floor exhibits focus on the establishment of Marietta, including General Putnam's original home built as a part of Fort Campus Martius and artifacts from the original settlement. The lower-level exhibits take a close look at the movement of people from farms to cities between 1850 and 1910, and from Appalachia into Ohio's industrial centers between 1910 and 1970.

Southwestern Ohio

In southwestern Ohio, the city of Cincinnati features many attractions for visitors. The second-oldest zoo in the country, the Cincinnati Zoo and Botanical Garden, is located there. It is ranked as one of the top five zoos in the United States. The Cincinnati Zoo is known for its cat collection, which includes white Bengal tigers. Cincinnati is also the hometown of the first major league baseball team, which was organized in 1866. The team is known today as the Cincinnati Reds.

Baseball fans cheer for the Cincinnati Reds in their hometown.

Paramount's Kings Island is located near Cincinnati. This park has the world's longest wooden roller coaster and a replica of the Eiffel Tower.

East of Cincinnati is the Serpent Mound. Located in Adams County, it is the largest and finest snake-shaped mound in the United States. Nearly a quarter of a mile long, Serpent Mound represents an uncoiling serpent. A museum at the site has exhibits about the mound and information about the surrounding area.

Farther north, near Dayton, is the Wright-Patterson Air Force Base. The field where the Wright Brothers built the first airplane is part of the base. The United States Air Force Museum is also located there. The museum tells the exciting story of aviation development from the days of the Wright brothers at Kitty Hawk to the Space Age. Exhibits include more than 300 aircraft.

Visiting places around the state not only helps us to understand the history of Ohio, it also offers us a glimpse into its future. It is likely that the hard work and creativity of Ohioans during the state's first 200 years will serve as inspiration for future generations.

Airplanes from World War II are on display at the United States Air Force Museum.

69

OHIO ALMANAC

Statehood date and number: March 1, 1803/17th

State seal: A sheaf of wheat and a cluster of seventeen arrows resembling a sheaf of wheat is in the foreground. In the background is a representation of Mount Logan, as viewed from the Adena State memorial. Over the mount is a rising sun with 17 rays (to represent Ohio as the 17th state) shining over the first state in the Northwest Territory. The outer portion of the rays form a semicircle. Created in 1803 and adopted in 1967.

State flag: The flag has a swallowtail shape. The large blue triangle represents Ohio's hills and valleys, and the stripes represent roads and waterways. The 13 stars grouped about the circle represent the original states of the union; the 4 stars added to the corner of the triangle symbolize that Ohio was the 17th state admitted to the union. The white circle with red center not only represents the "O" in Ohio but also suggests Ohio's famous nickname, the Buckeye State. Adopted in 1902.

Geographic center: Centerburg, in Knox County

Total area/rank: 44,828 square miles (116,104 sq km)/34th

Borders: Lake Erie, Michigan, Kentucky, West Virginia, Pennsylvania, and Indiana

Latitude and longitude: Ohio is located approximately between 38° 27' and 41° 57' N and 80° 34' and 84° 49' W

Highest/lowest elevation: Campbell Hill in Logan County, 1,549 feet (472 m) above sea level/the Ohio River near Cincinnati, 455 feet (139 m) above sea level

Hottest/coldest temperature: 113°F (45°C) near Gallipolis on July 21, 1934/−39°F (−39.4°C) at Milligan on February 10, 1899

Land area/rank: 40,953 square miles (106,068 sq km)/35th

Inland water area/rank: 376 square miles (974 sq km)

Population/rank (2000 census): 11,353,140/7th

Population of major cities (2000 census):
  Columbus: 711,470
  Cleveland: 478,403
  Cincinnati: 331,285
  Toledo: 313,619
  Akron: 217,074

Origin of state name: Derived from Iroquois word meaning "great river" or "beautiful river"

State capital: Columbus

Previous capitals: Chillicothe, Zanesville

Counties: 88

State government: 33 senators, 99 representatives

Major rivers/lakes: Ohio River, Miami River, Scioto River, and Muskingum River/Pymatuning Reservoir, Grand Lake, Berlin, Indian, Mosquito Creek, and Senecaville Lakes

Farm products: Soybeans, corn, soft red winter wheat, hothouse vegetables, tomatoes, apples, and grapes

Livestock: Hogs, cattle, and sheep

Manufactured products: Transportation equipment including airplane engines, auto parts, and motorcycles; also machinery construction, sheet metal, steel, aluminum, and soap products

Mining products: Coal, clay, sand, gravel, limestone, and salt

Animal: White-tailed deer

Beverage: Tomato juice

Bird: Cardinal

Flower: Red carnation

Fossil: Isoletus, commonly known as the trilobite. This now-extinct sea creature existed in Ohio 440 million years ago, when saltwater covered the state. It resembles the modern horseshoe crab and is about 14 inches (36 cm) long.

Gemstone: Flint

Insect: Ladybug

Motto: "With God All Things Are Possible"

Nickname: Buckeye State

Reptile: Black racer snake

Rock Song: "Hang on Sloopy"

Song: "Beautiful Ohio," words by Ballard MacDonald, music by Mary Earl

Tree: The Buckeye

Wildflower: *Trillium grandiflorum,* commonly known as the large white trillium

Wildlife: White-tailed deer, beavers, raccoons, skunks, fox, muskrats, migrating ducks, terns, gulls, sparrows, blue rays, and cardinals

TIMELINE

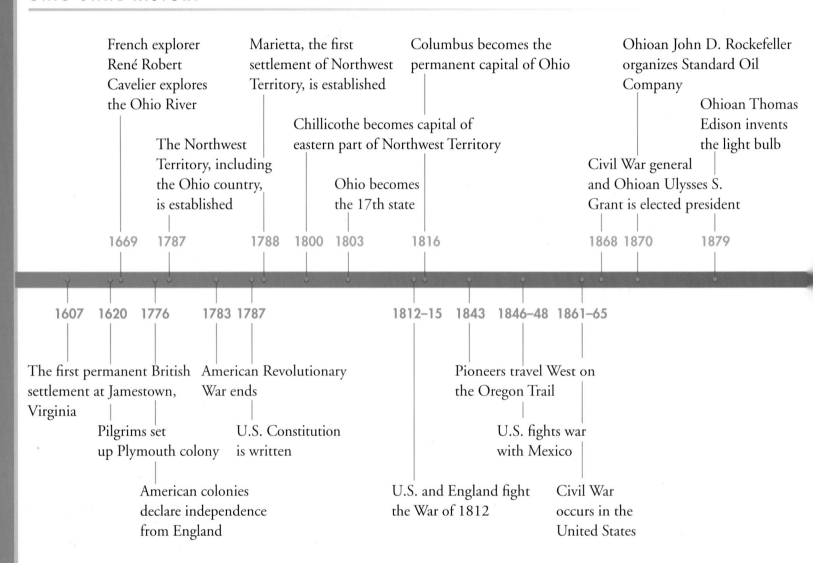

French explorer René Robert Cavelier explores the Ohio River

Marietta, the first settlement of Northwest Territory, is established

Columbus becomes the permanent capital of Ohio

Ohioan John D. Rockefeller organizes Standard Oil Company

Ohioan Thomas Edison invents the light bulb

The Northwest Territory, including the Ohio country, is established

Chillicothe becomes capital of eastern part of Northwest Territory

Ohio becomes the 17th state

Civil War general and Ohioan Ulysses S. Grant is elected president

1669 1787   1788 1800 1803   1816   1868 1870   1879

1607 1620 1776   1783 1787   1812–15 1843 1846–48 1861–65

The first permanent British settlement at Jamestown, Virginia

American Revolutionary War ends

Pioneers travel West on the Oregon Trail

Pilgrims set up Plymouth colony

U.S. Constitution is written

U.S. fights war with Mexico

American colonies declare independence from England

U.S. and England fight the War of 1812

Civil War occurs in the United States

UNITED STATES HISTORY

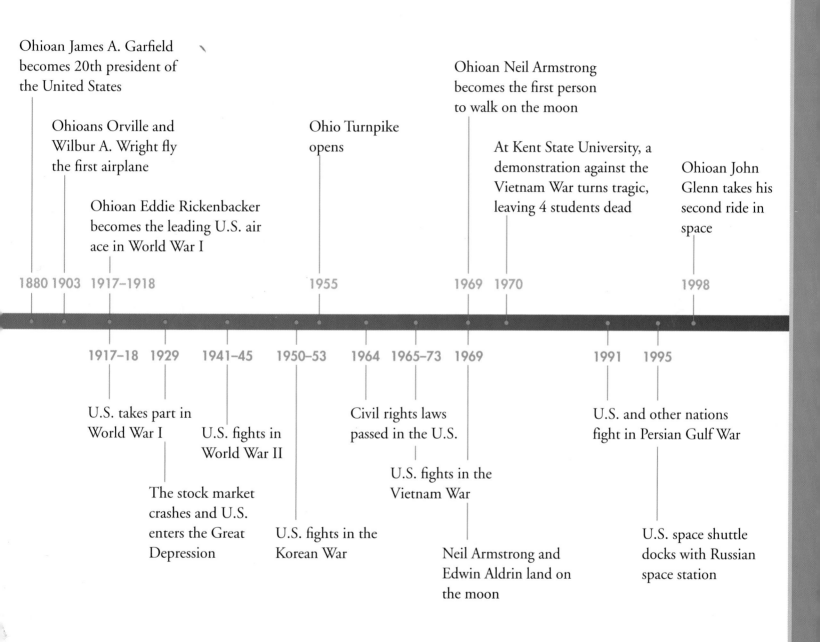

Ohioan James A. Garfield becomes 20th president of the United States

Ohioans Orville and Wilbur A. Wright fly the first airplane

Ohioan Eddie Rickenbacker becomes the leading U.S. air ace in World War I

Ohio Turnpike opens

Ohioan Neil Armstrong becomes the first person to walk on the moon

At Kent State University, a demonstration against the Vietnam War turns tragic, leaving 4 students dead

Ohioan John Glenn takes his second ride in space

1880 1903 1917–1918   1955   1969 1970   1998

1917–18 1929   1941–45   1950–53   1964   1965–73   1969   1991   1995

U.S. takes part in World War I

U.S. fights in World War II

Civil rights laws passed in the U.S.

U.S. and other nations fight in Persian Gulf War

U.S. fights in the Vietnam War

The stock market crashes and U.S. enters the Great Depression

U.S. fights in the Korean War

Neil Armstrong and Edwin Aldrin land on the moon

U.S. space shuttle docks with Russian space station

GALLERY OF FAMOUS OHIOANS

George Armstrong Custer

(1839–1876)

An American soldier. His "Last Stand" against Sioux and Cheyenne warriors at the Battle of Little Bighorn in Montana (1876) has become a legend in American history. Born in New Rumley.

John Glenn

(1921–)

First U.S. astronaut to orbit the earth (1962) and the oldest astronaut ever to go into space (1998). Also a U.S. senator from Ohio (1975–1999). Born in Cambridge.

Virginia Hamilton

(1936–2002)

Award-winning children's book author. She won a Newbery medal for her book, *M.C. Higgins the Great*. Born in Yellow Springs.

John Mercer Langston

(1829–1897)

Believed to have been the first African-American elected to public office in 1854 when he was elected clerk of Brownhelm. He grew up in Ohio.

Toni Morrison

(1931–)

First African-American woman to receive the Nobel Prize (1993) in literature. Born in Lorain.

Judith Resnik

(1949–1986)

Second American woman in space. She died on January 28, 1986 on board the *Challenger*, which exploded shortly after launch. Born in Akron.

Steven Spielberg

(1946–)

Hollywood's most successful film director and producer. Born in Cincinnati.

Lillian Wald

(1867–1940)

Started world's first public-school nursing program and co-founded the Visiting Nurses Service. Born in Cincinnati.

Victoria Claflin Woodhull

(1838–1927)

First woman to run for president of the United States, in 1872. Born in Homer.

Granville Woods

(1856–1910)

Inventor of more than 35 devices, including a telegraph machine that could transmit messages from one moving train to another. Born in Columbus.

GLOSSARY

allocate: to distribute or assign

artificial: made by humans

circumference: the distance around a circle

controversy: a prolonged or heated debate

domestic: relating to a household or a family

drench: to wet thoroughly

elevation: height above sea level

erosion: the gradual wearing away of land due to wind, rain, or ice

fertile: producing much vegetation

frost: a covering of tiny ice crystals on a cold surface

humid: moist

interactive: active between people, groups, or things

juvenile: relating to children or young people

metropolitan: relating to a city

migration: the act of moving from one region to another

modify: to make changes

obligation: something that requires one to do something

pollution: the act of making something unclean, such as air or water

prohibited: not allowed something

successive: a series of persons or things that follow one another

FOR MORE INFORMATION

Web sites

http://www.oplin.lib.oh.us/products/ohiodefined/symbols.html
O-HI-O Defined. Provides information about the state symbols of Ohio.

http://www.ohiotourism.com
The web site for Ohio Tourism, with information about attractions and events.

http://www.oplin.lib.oh.us/
Ohio Public Library Information Network. Provides links to a variety of internet sites relating to all aspects of Ohio, including history, current events, and a web site for kids.

http://www.americaslibrary.gov/cgi-bin/page.cgi
America's Story from America's Library (hosted by the Library of Congress). Stories about the development of America, including the states.

Books

Bial, Raymond. *Amish Home.* New York, NY: Houghton Mifflin Co., 1993.

Christopher, Debbonnaire. *The Day the Ohio Canal Turned Eerie.* Coshocton, OH: Roscoe Village Foundation, 1993.

Gallant, Roy. *Glaciers* (First Book Series). Danbury, CT: Franklin Watts, 1999.

Bial, Raymond. *The Underground Railroad.* New York, NY: Houghton Mifflin Co., 1995.

Isham, Bruce. *Johnny Appleseed.* Bandicoot Books, 1998.

Addresses

Governor of Ohio
30th Floor
77 South High Street
Columbus, OH 43215-6117

Ohio Department of Development
77 S. High Street
P. O. Box 1001
Columbus, OH 43216-1001

Ohio Department of Natural Resources
1952 Belcher Drive, Building C
Columbus, OH 43224-1386

INDEX

ABOUT THE AUTHOR

Nancy Kline lives in northwest Ohio. She began free-lance writing in 1974 and has published numerous works, including greeting cards and activity books. She has also served as editor of a county newspaper.

Nancy and her husband Keith traveled to various places in Ohio to research this book. Nancy enjoys writing to make history come alive for children. "History is more than dates and wars," she said. "It's about people. That is why I enjoyed writing this book on Ohio so much. It was fun to find out more about the people of Ohio."

Photographs © 2002: AP/Wide World Photos/Daniel Miller: 61; Archive Photos/Getty Images/Bernard Gotfryd: 74 bottom left; Corbis Images: 74 right (AFP), 35, 42, 45 background, 62 (Bettman), 19 (Richard A. Cooke), 40 (Kevin Fleming), 48 (Charles O'Rear), 38 (Charles E. Rotkin), 67 (UPI), 28, 29, 36, 65; Dembinsky Photo Assoc./John Mielcarek: 71 bottom left; Folio, Inc.: 68 (David R. Frazier Photolibrary), 69 (Jeff Greenberg@juno.com), 49 (Dennis Johnson); H. Armstrong Roberts, Inc.: cover, 9 (J. Blank), 71 top left (R. Roper), 3 left, 14 (W.J. Scott), 12 (F. Sieb); Ian Adams Photography: 10, 70 right; MapQuest.com, Inc.: 70 bottom left; NASA: 74 top left; New England Stock Photo/Jean Higgins: 53; North Wind Picture Archives: 17, 20, 21, 22, 23 top, 23 bottom, 26, 27, 59; Ohio Bicentennial Commission/Joe Murray: 41; Randall L. Schieber: 31, 43, 56; Root Resources: 3 right, 63 (Claudia Adams), 52 (Larry Schaefer); Stock Montage, Inc.: 24, 32 bottom, 32 top, 33 bottom; Stone/Getty Images/Andy Sacks: 57; Superstock, Inc.: 4, 7, 33 top, 34, 55, 66; Tom Till: 8, 16; Unicorn Stock Photos/Martha McBride: 71 bottom right; Visuals Unlimited/Arthur R. Hill: 71 top right.

GAYLORD R